AF368562

Shine like a Phoenix

Shefali Lal

Published by

TANEESHA PUBLISHERS

BOOK PUBLISH.IN

Title   :   Shine Like a Phoenix
Author   :   Shefali Lal
Editor   :   Tushar Gautam
Edition   :   1st (November, 2023)
ISBN   :   978-8119580828

© 2023, All Rights Reserved by Author under Indian Copyright Act 1957

Published by

In Association with

Regd. Add.: Taneesha Publishers, 254, Khuriyakhatta No. 10, Bindukhatta, Lalkuan, Nainital - 262402, Uttarakhand, India
Website : www.taneeshapublishers.in
E-mail : taneeshapublishers@gmail.com
Phone : +91 845481 2712, +91 976041 7980

Cover Design & Interior Layout by : **BookPublish.in**

Printed by : Manipal Technologies Limited, Bengaluru - 560001

COPYRIGHT NOTICE & PUBLISHER DISCLAIMER

Copyright rights of this book including compositions, descriptions, statements, opinions included in this book are reserved by the author, so no any part of this book shall be reproduced partially electronic or mechanical (including film, serial, photographic, without the written permission of the author Recording, any newspaper, magazine, literary portal news portal, blog or translation into another language) in any manner whatsoever without written permission from the author, except in the case of brief quotations embodied in critical articles and reviews. If a person or institution attempts to do so, they will be responsible for the legal action.

Disclaimer : This book has been published with all efforts taken to make the material error-free after the consent of the author. However, the author and the publisher do not assume and hereby disclaim any liability to any party for any loss, damage, or disruption caused by errors or omissions, whether such errors or omissions result from negligence, or any other cause. While every effort has been made to avoid any mistake or omission, this publication is being sold on the condition and understanding that neither the author nor the publishers or printers would be liable in any manner to any person by reason of any mistake or omission in this publication or for any action taken or omitted to be taken or advice rendered or accepted on the basis of this work. For any defect in printing or binding, the publisher will be liable only to replace the defective copy by another copy of this book then available through the same seller or distributor where purchased it.

Shine Like a Phoenix

Shefali Lal

(Author)

INDEX

Editorial

Dear Reader,

We hope you will definitely like this book. This book has been published for the purpose of contributing to the literature in the field of literature. Continuous literary publication is a need of today's time. To take Indian literature to its legendary status, continuous support and cooperation of the reader along with the author and the publisher is also necessary. You are making this literary work of ours meaningful by reading this book of ours.

It is taking our society in a better, new, and modern

direction. This book is also available in digital form. By publishing books on digital platforms, we are contributing somewhere not only on the path of technology but also in the field of environmental protection. This is a small beginning;

Along with protecting the environment, and helping people publish their literature. We hope that through this book you will be able to connect with the thoughts and feelings of the writer.

Please send your feedback to us and the writer through print and digital mediums.

Tushar Gautam

(Editor)

www.BookPublish.in

We Worth It

I always feel unhappy

Why I was not allowed to sing?

There is a question on my upbringing

Why I was not allowed

attending late-night parties?

Sitting alone eating vegetable Frankies

Why I was not considered beautiful

Not destined to be free and cheerful.

Designated by the terms 'Submissive'

and 'Inferior 'Not to feel ambitious and superior.

Now it's the time to move on

Like a burn-the-bra feminist

Stand with poise and do justice

Change the fucking perception of society

Existence of a woman is not a topic of anxiety

Let's celebrate the epitome of beauty with brain

Throw all the debris of stereotypes down the drain.

✎ Shefali Lal

Being an HIV

Being an HIV it's a complicated thing

Feels like someone reluctantly cut our wings.

I used to be a multifaceted personality

God knows where the virus comes uninvitedly.

I used to dance, sing, and swing

My boyfriend dumped me

and returned the engagement ring

I loved to cook and eat pancakes

Now I feel disgusted on growing eyelashes.

I used to run fast like a winner of marathon

Now I become lazy and lethargic like a sloth.

Completely unaware of the symptoms

of unprotected sex

Condoms and lubricants makes me vex

Friends and relatives make a distance from me

Labelled with the terms 'Outcast',

'Untouchable' and 'Nasty '

Not allowed to take a bite of fruits which are juicy

Want to escape from this gruesome reality

Bring guilt, pain and suffering to humanity.

It's a misconception that it's contagious

Stop pretending that you are intelligent and factious

Give a passionate kiss and warm hug who are needy

They also have the right to love freely.

Shefali Lal

Break the Silence

Have you ever seen yourself?

Look like a swollen duckling

Honey you don't need to be jealous

Poor thing you never look stunning.

You always act foolish

Don't know how to lure a man

Please get me a bowl of porridge

Apply sunscreen on body tan.

You always lack intellect

Don't know how to use birth control pills?

Completely pissed off and have no respect

Seems like abandoned and jilt.

Oh! You forgot to put the icing on the cake

It's a part of your household chore

Please forgive me for god sake

Deliberately I don't close the door.

Don't be intimidated,

When I stripped another woman

You are supposed to be quiet and calm

Behave yourself in front of another gentleman

Being naked will not take your charm.

Please close the door, while you leave

It disturbs me and my beloved

Your unwanted tears will not make me naive

Undoubtedly you will be ignored and snubbed.

Excuse me, I am your wife, not a slave

Stop giving me instructions like a master

I am independent, sassy, and brave

Thanks for your unappealing gesture.

 Shefali Lal

Unidentified

In my couch, I was lying

and involved with my thoughts

That is why some special people

in society suffer a lot?

People who deserve to be caressed

and loved the most

society wholeheartedly laugh

and make them roast.

Is it wrong to be a lesbian or gay?

Why should we isolate us from their way?

Individuality has been deeply shaken

Identity of a human also need a patent.

Last night, I kissed a gay

Parents said that you have no shame

I was about to be assaulted by a stranger

Hopefully, saved by a lesbian singer.

Appreciate what you are ,believe what you can

Every individual is unique

and beautiful in their own aspect

Respect and Love the LGBTQ community

Prove the real meaning of unity in diversity.

Shefali Lal

It's Good to be Cuckold

I am not going to tell, do whatever you want

You can slammed and slapped me.

Will shut my mouth and smile like a pro

Throw the key of my dark secrets in silent sea.

I am not going to tell, no. of my affairs

You can rub my head against the wall .

Walk like a slut with no shame

Having wine in my hand, dance on rocks.

I am not going to tell, the place where I hooked up

You can strangulate me with my hair .

Show my curves, under my clothes

Bent down confidently sitting on choir.

I am not going to tell, where I have kept

my diary of lustful stories

You can break my fingers.

Gently whispered in my lover ears

Beneath the blanket without any langereis.

Why I can't be cuckold? Does it suits to only man

Where the stereotypes and misogynists gone?

Hidden their face into quilt

Break the detestable gender biased rules

Those who cheated on their partners

deserved to be guilt and jilt.

— Shefali Lal

Laughter is Silent

Laughter is Silent

I am violent.

Isolation and loneliness now my friends

I don't want to attend any fests.

Some scars are inexplicable and incurable

Human problems are inevitable.

Aspirations and dreams are now

become nightmare

Feels disinterested attending fares.

Medicines and therapies

failed to work as stress buster

I lost my charm and lustre .

Wandering around feelings of

hatred and arrogance

Awfully crying for being ignorant.

Misery and pain are intangible to people

Don't know where I have lost my slippers?

Unworthiness killing me

Where I have lost my happiness key?

I am scared and afraid

Rays of enthusiasm

and excitement are going to fade .

Seems like that I doesn't belong to this world

Feels dejected and absurd.

No worries,

If you are not successful and happy

No worries ,

If you look little flabby

No worries,

If you lost your love

No worries,

If you have problem of personality disorder

Spread your wings like an albatross

Shine, love, and laugh by

saying "Praise the lord".

✒ Shefali Lal

Unfulfilled Dreams

Have you ever cried in alone?

There is not a success stone .

Dreaming of a successful career

Wishing to be a untamed chariot.

Torned shoes tearful eyes

Why the sun sets again rise?

We are wandering here and there

Saving money, because father is not here.

Lesser grades poor marks

Again I lost my chance .

No matter at any cost I will fight

One day success of kite will fly.

Life is full of surprises

Stepping back dwell into crisis .

Weeping and sobbing it's not a solution

Dreams are fulfilled without a resolution.

Shefali Lal

Dying Spirit

Why we are dying?

Because of stressful life .

Again and again choking ourselves

Let us handle the situation themselves.

As it leaves a body, spirit is free

Why you are mischievous and freak?

People die not of prolonged disease and accidents

Occurs due to lack of emotions and sentiments.

I don't know what's the reason ?

Digging a grave for fake treason .

Manipulated childhood and licentious adulthood

Tell me the address of good parenthood.

Are you weak or timid?

Giving up your spirit

Wait for a moment, Time has come

Awake your spirit, Everyone has to suffer.

Not to lose hope and faith

Just wish and pray .

Heal, Relief, and enlightenment

Dying spirit will sing in joy and excitement.

Shefali Lal

Dusky Beauty

Whenever I saw myself in the mirror

I run in awe and terror.

My little sister is plump and fair

I was not allowed to sit in the chair.

I go to school with an anxious mind

Are you going to be a friend of mine?

Being bold and beautiful was a question

Color complexity can worsen the situation.

My mother restrict me, wearing a skirt

Why should I consider myself as slut?

Applying peeling mask and fairness cream

For the society sake and

becoming someone's dream?

Being beautiful seems terrible for me

It's my right to be childish and fly free .

Toxic relationships give guilt and pain

Having irrestible beauty goes in vain.

Beauty with brain is the gift of God.

My father beat with a rod .

Day by day, growing weak and pale

You are supposed to fail.

I never felt disappointed for a single moment

Again I lost my golden bracelet and locket.

I will rise, I will shine at any cost

One day, I will wear a tiara of pride and boast.

Shefali Lal

Prayer in Brothel

At the age of 15,with skinny body

I was playing in the lobby.

Chided and rebuked and called off from School

Instructed to clean the house with broom.

Achievements and accomplishments

are not for me

As a girl, I was not destined to be free.

A perfect gentleman make a bid

And I was forced to go into that shit.

Don't be ashamed of your nakedness

It won't be going to stained your greatness.

Beautiful and curvaceous

figure are always welcomed

Ready to put yourself first to be sanctioned.

Should I give upon sex?

It's your duty be bold and frank.

Showing skinny legs to a stranger

Fuck my body like a scavenger.

Sleepless nights and sagging eyes

Hold on I am so tired .

My body shivers in cold and pain

They have no guilt and shame.

Prayer in brothel are you kidding?

It's not a place for this type of bullshitting.

Let's pray together for resurrection and rebirth

Jesus, don't give me the labour pain

of illegitimate Child birth.

Shefali Lal

Be Like a Badass

Why shouldn't I write?

To prove ourselves we have to fight.

Like my brother, I am also intelligent

Just stop it, and be Silent.

Oh, it's quite dark stay at home

Mama, I also want to go for a trip in Rome.

Mind is filled with unexpected misfortunes

Give me the chance to play a melodious tune.

Don't wear such revealing top

Walk slowly, don't hop.

Be simple and sober that's the feminity

Bad guys want to take your virginity.

Delay in periods, something is wrong?

Mama is standing holding a tong .

Hide and seek with justifications

and clarifications

I want to run from these

fucking accusations.

Live like a badass, not an issue

I don't wipe my tears with tissue.

It's my choice not an option

Self -reliance and self worth

are not the things for auction.

    Shefali Lal

Shine Like a Phoenix

Why we are so disheartened?

Just because of failures and heartbreaks.

Become furious and agitated

Brutally trolled among group of friends.

All our efforts would go in vain

That makes us troublesome and anxious.

One of dear ones has been

the patient of migrane.

And we are inclined to become factious.

Always censored and

criticized for our misdeeds

Left with a broken heart and hollow mind .

Even unconditional love

and affection are also charged not free

Not supposed to dream big and on cloud nine.

Not everyone is born with a silver spoon

Chasing behind for fame and fortune.

Alas! Not destined to shine like a moon

You are not for me and I am not for you.

Nonetheless, don't care what people think

Not to feel offended and disheartened.

Fall and Rise, Fall and Rise smile with a blink

Shine like a Phoenix and grab your success back.

  Shefali Lal

That Long Uncommunication

Why I have tears in my eyes?

Seems like everything is going to be finish .

Everyone has pretended to be nice

My love for you is true not a fling.

I can't able to sleep properly

Mind is continuously wavering

around your memories.

Disconnected from you unwillingly

I am stuck between longing loveand

an unending financial crisis.

Today, I have no identity, not an issue

Bad luck stabbed me on my back.

Is it my fault that I never tasted

that expensive cashew?

Left with no pennies in my bank.

Long gap in Communication

gives me the strength

To be the best version of myself.

Not a joke that they feel discontent

Why should I suffer alone and feel helpless?

One day, My path breaking success will

become the strongest evidence

Become restless to know

the address of my residence.

Feel sorry and guilty

for their unfavorable gesture

Think thousand times to take

a such step in future.

Shefali Lal

My Lipstick is not Red

What the hell we do to deserve this? This poor fucking old man for his own lascivious and promiscuous needs use our body, torment our soul, Don't know when it's going to be end? Is the God become blindfolded? Is it Pre -destined for all the girls and women become the puppet in patriarchal society? These blistering questions hovered upon two girls, who become helpless and continuously blaming their destiny who sacrificed their teenagehood for the sake of of bread and butter.

Sara and Laura are twins. After giving birth to Laura, their mother died. Their eccentric and insolent father shifted both little ones into an orphanage to get rid of them as he was unhappy and unsatisfied with birth of two girls. Both the twins grew in nurturing, pampered, serene environment of orphanage but feeling of despondence, desolation, and disappointment always made them acknowledge of being parentless.

It's always said that misfits and misfortunes come to an end at one point. Unfortunately, this seems to be contradictory and conflicting in the case of these twins. One day, something unexpected happened when the new orphan keeper took the charge of Happy Little Angels Orphanage home. Mrs. Sandra Chadwick, is a heartless lady, whose sternness and rigourness of her face gives a glance of the character of Mrs. Reed in the novel 'Jane Eyre'.

Mrs. Chadwick was a cold -hearted lady, affection, pity, compassion, kindness, and humanity, seem to be vanished and disappeared in her dictionary. She never left a chance to bully and humiliate children, always ready to make a mountain out of a molehill.

Nonetheless, Sara and Laura were also severely ill treated by her. When both sisters entering into 13th year, they got their 1st period ,situation becomes more worsened and drastic. They were denied of using sanitary pads by Mrs. Chadwick as according to her, it would cause bacterial infection which was none other the another way to lead one a pretty dance. Excessive flows in midnights make the twins exasperated. Happy Little Angels orphanage now turned into Sorrow and frustration Little Angels.

All the children of the orphanage realized that serene, happy, comfortable environment of orphanage now turned into a lifelong confinement. Memories of happy childhood suddenly becomes a nightmare. Sara and Laura compelled to work like washing utensils, cleaning the floors of each and every room ,cutting and slicing the vegetables. At the age of them when other children hold pencils, erasers, books disheartened twins with tears rolling over their eyes cutting and slicing, peeling the vegetables and fruits. Other children begged that atleast on weekends, they could play, dance, and sing and do whatever their longed and desired it seems like God unheard the prayers of these innocent souls.

'I am totally pissed off. Why should I again and again peeling the vegetables and fruits even if it already done?. We are entangled in the web which is interwoven by this witch and doesn't know when we would be able to breath in fresh air".Laura said to Sara while preparing the food for the dinner. Sara was more tolerant and submissive than Laura. She always try to calm down her sister nerves as she was quiet apprehensive that both of them would lost roofs on their head.

Mrs. Chadwick had a eagle eye on both sisters ,and always looking for an opportunity to snare the noose around their neck Her endless series of fucking instructions, rebuking and scolding the children unnecessarily and deliberately in her sheer screeching voice ultimately intensify the emotions of turbulence and perturbation.

It's old adage that ''good things come in disguise form'', injustice, violence, tormentation, sometimes makes a victim vulnerable to take an action which would make the victimizer dumbfounded.

One day, Sara as usual cleaning the floor. Meanwhile,some portion of floor cleaner were spread out on the floor as its cap was little bit loosened. At the moment, Mrs. Chadwick come hurriedly and loses her balance and fell down. Sara who was engaged in her work, become shocked and scared that what was happened. Her heartbeat becomes faster than the speed of F1 cars. She feels like she was was about to dying in a nasty pit. Her fingers throbbed in terror.

' What the fuck is going on? Mrs. Chadwick shouted and then gathering her strength manage herself to stand. Her eyes become red, as it was a massive volcanic eruption. Furious and annoyed, She leaned towards Sara and said 'You scoundrel nasty pig, have you lose your mind? Damn you are 14 yrs old now and you didn't know to tighten the cap of a bottle?. Thanks to Jesus, that I didn't broken my ribs.

Sara stands like a mannequin, frightened and scared replied hesitantly 'Sorry, I didn't do intentionally. Actually I am quite feverish today ,and didn't get the time to take medicines. Mrs. Chadwick presence was not less of a hag or witch like in gothic or horror movies. Her tall, skinny personality with stern features and voice could scared even a bird or rat.

'Stop telling your fabricated stories, they won't work for out for me. You are becoming irresponsible day by day, and now you have to pay for this what you have done '. Mrs. Chadwick firmly gripped her hand.

Hopeless and innocent Sara was shaken and startled in terror and fear. Her heart was squeezed and shrinked like a flat balloon. That was the last straw, which intrigued her sister, who was watching the whole incident. She vehemently protested and boldly warned Mrs..Chadwick to release her sister's hand.

'Don't to dare to give warning to me, Another Nasty Pig, You are not different from your sister. Both of you, should give credit to me for my kindness and generosity, for providing shelter and meal to you.

'Credit? Laura answered with a smirky and sarcastic smile, 'Of course All the children of this orphanage including us will give you credit for your ruthless and savage gesture. We will give credit to you for snatching the memories of childhood of parentless and hopeless orphans, who are forced to live in flithy and choked environment of so called of this orphanage. And why these children even both siblings are thankful and grateful to you for giving stale and leftover food instead of fresh food which is ultimately prepared by us, but unfortunately it is fault in our stars to take a even single bite of it. We are overwhelmed by your fucking benevolence and mercy that pushed us into utter disgrace.

At the end of conversation ,Laura said to Sara with mournful eyes 'Let's run from this bullshit. And both twins holding hands escaped like two antelopes after being free from the clutches of hungry and blood -thirsty Lion.

After being emancipated from the web of unjust

authority and suppressing atmosphere, Both twins felt relieved and relaxed. Both of them take a deep sigh as like big enormous rock were displaced and dislodged from their chest. However they were quite disappointed that they didn't help other children to become free from that bullshit imprisonment but they firmly believed that they set an example against the unjust misconduct and unfair authority of a malicious and malignant lady.

Sometimes decisions make in rash or in fit make us to comprehend and stepped back in deep contemplation whether the decision made was appropriate or not. Unbearable hunger of stomach, hot scorching rays of sunlight, perpetual threat of being sexually abused by any unwelcomed person, undoubtedly fly away the idealized views . Wandering in the streets, begging to walk in restaurants, to afford meals ,torned clothes and slippers with hopeless eyes and shattered heart makes twins pathetic and miserable.

Eagerness and excitement of two teenage twins to start a new journey of freedom and liberty now turned into debris of Misery, Pain, disappointment and guilt. Intense hunger make them reluctant to go back into that pit. Unacceptable climatic conditions compelled to step back and unwillingly fell down in front of that fucking orphan keeper. But whatever the situation was, both twins stand through thick and thin.

After several days of struggle with hunger and unbearable heatwaves, they finally got the accommodation provided by a old man named Mr. Stalin.

It's old adage that "Don't judge a book by its cover". Never trust blindly on unknown person extreme kindness and generosity as it could be concealed and disclosed under the thin sheets made up of dark colours.

There was something peculiar and quirky about Mr. Stalin. An old man, with a stout body, living in the outskirts of New York City was an embodiment of unwonted and abnormal traits. In the age of 50 -55, he was living lonely in a duplex apartment without any security.

His wife had been deceased 10 yrs back, when he served as a civilian employee in government His eldest daughter had been married to a Army officer who were living in Chicago and his other daughter gone to abroad for higher studies. His son, who was youngest among three, always spend money like a rich spoilt brat. His expenditure on luxurious branded clothes, wines, Cars, higlilghts the exaggeration and extravagance of rich sons who never feel ounce of shame and guilty, who never and ever come forward to help those who struggled and find difficulty to manage for two times. A son of retired civilian servant heart never goes out to know the whereabouts of his lonely father.

However, it was quite noteworthy that besides his Son, Mr. Stalin's daughters never telephoned him, never make an effort to meet him or spend some quality time with him. All that was in 2-3 months, both of them made a video call, and even in video chat they made innumerable ways of pretending that the connection was cut, speed of the internet was slow or the server of the laptop was down so they would call through cellphone.

Nonetheless, whatever the reality was, clouds of misconception and misapprehension were going to be cleared very soon and give a uttermost sensation just like hot lava chocolate cake. One day, Sara as usual making a tea for Mr. Stalin. It was 7:30 of Sunday morning.

She wore a floral midi normal slippers. Mr. Stalin woke up around 9 , rubbing his eyes, wore his nightrobe went down by the stairs, holding his clothes and morning routine products,Suddenly his eyes were struck on the flourishing beauty of Sara. It seems like that he loses his senses, licking his lips, cracking his fingers comes closer to her and makes a hay while the sun shines.

'Why are you doing here, Mr. Stalin, I mean anything you want? Sara got herself in work that she didn't feel the presence around her.

Mr. Stalin, with deep introspective eyes, gives a very eccentric and whimsical smile, scrutinizing her body from head to toe. The most disgusting and disgraceful thing was that his malicious eyes were stopped at her boobs.

'Nothing, Mr. Stalin, replied in a clumsy manner. 'Can I ask a question to you sweetie? If you don't mind? '.'Yeah sure, why not? Sara replied in low voice.

He come closer to her and stand without any space of air and whispered in her ears 'Have you ever sex with someone? If not then I can make your dream come true. You are looking so gorgeous, that I can't get my eyes off. Come to my bedroom after lunch.

The foundation of trust, humility, respect, modesty were fallen down like a pack of cards. Innocent ,downtrodden Sara were seems to be perplexed, looking down into the floor with guilt and pain. She doesn't what was going to happened if she refused to become fucking sex partner of this licentious old man. She feels like she was standing in the midst of battlefield where the fight was between her virginity and voluptuous hunger, between gratification of sexual desires and modesty and humility of two harmless souls.

Both loving twins Sara and Laura were used by Mr. Stalin like puppets There was not a single day left when they were not inappropriately touched or stared by him. In case of Mrs. Chadwick they strongly opposed of her ill treatment but in Mr. Stalin Casey it seems befitting for them as he was prestigious retired civil servant, any protest or oppose could fall them into an awkward situation. Whenever, they make a step forward for stopping these fucking indulgence in sexual gratification they become scared with the thought of deprived them from shelter and food. They started cursing their god that the sins of whom and why were beholded to them?

Perhaps, doesn't matter what was going around minds of both were preoccupied with hope, and sanguiness. There was still rays of light of resurrection, rebirth, and resurgence which was quite enough to burn all all the uncertainties and complexities of life.

Finally the anticipation of both siblings were come true. They were free themselves from being sex toys of that fucking licentious old man. An women activist ,Mrs. Thorndike come their help and got arrested Mr. Stalin for sexual abuse of teenage twins. Both twins got admitted in school so they complete their studies. They feel obliged and glad for Mrs Thorndike unconditional love and and support as she come into their life like an Angel.

One day, Laura was getting ready for annual function and she was about to put dark red matte lipstick but interrupted by Sara, as she was quite uncontented for applying a red lipstick in school function but Laura with full determination and confidence replied that 'Okay sis I will minimize the quantity of it, but I will not rub it any cost because this is not merely a beauty or cosmetic product ,but it's a symbol of passion indomitable confidence, unsurmountable sassiness, unbeatable strength of every woman of this universe. This red colour makes me and you acknowledged that every aspect of life has a bright and beautiful side of it. It revitalizes and rejunvates our lives with beautiful colours of liberty, freedom and independence.

Shefali Lal

Unfruitful Tolerance

What do you think you can easily fool me? Stop straining your nerves in unnecessary thinking, do what suits you better, doing household chores, taking care of children in laws what makes you a beautiful typical Indian woman.

Sharda husband ,Arun comes from a elite family, a successful businessman, gold medalist in state level, but unfortunately a business tycoon never make a effort to unlocked the aspirations, hopes, feelings, of her poor downtrodden wife whose spirit was entangled in sheets of endless responsibilties of household chores.

Before marriage, unlike other girls, Sharda was

quite adventurous Bob hairstyle, having a wardrobe of gents wear, hanging around her male friends, engaging herself in activities like hiking, trekking all over she was a Tomboy. Her personality was somewhat unacceptable in terms of societal norms, but at the same time, it would be wrong to say that behind the bold and presumptuous persona, there was a longing desire for true love.

At the time of marriage, She was only 25, left her studies drop out of her college, being married at that stage when people let their dreams fly in limitless sky, put their heart and soul for flourishing their career, Sharda become a well trained housewife and nurturing mother of two kids.

A girl who is embodiment of courage, determination,

and boldness was not destined to be subdued and ordered by anyone, Although she used to constant scolding by her parents and teachers, Sharda unwillingness and reluctance for surrendering herself works like a icing on the cake.

Being submissive and tolerant, was not a problem but what is most intriguing and intimidating is that the society never make a effort, become inconsiderate and insolent for recognizing the embedded qualities of a woman ,who is intelligent, diligent and become a pathbreaker in their respective field. Arun's domineering and bossy attitude, his hostility and callousness towards the women, nonetheless makes Sharda hollow and timid soul.

There was not a single day left when the screaming

and scorching unbearable voice of his husband, unheard by the neighbours. 'Why do you put less salt in Rice '? Why do you not wash my that yellow shirt, You have gained weight, try to cut it the office colleagues come in our house for a party.

All that stuff, becomes instrumental for creation of a boring monotonous and gloomy environment, a environment in which the control button o a pathetic woman was in the hands of his beloved husband. Her conceptualisation of ideas, her thought process to mend the things in her own way, was completed restricted and prohibited.

But one day, something unexpected was going to happened. Something that would create a history for the emancipation of a tormented soul. As usual,

Sharda husband was leaving for his office, but at the last moment he struggled in searching for his important file. All the frustration, arrogance, was directed towards his wife, Annoyed from head to toe, Arun shouted at his wife 'Why the hell, do you do in absence of mine? Can't you properly managed the things, You are good for nothing. This unbearable line makes Sharda moved to take a action rather than retreat back.

Her soul unshivered and stand out against all the odds of societal norms, She replied with full confidence, determination, 'Yes, I am not good for nothing, because I am a woman, a wife, a mother. Unlike you, I was not born after 9 months of pregnancy, My mother not suffered labor pain because she knew well that she was going to give birth a baby girl. When I was born, I was not crying because girls are destined for a painful suffering. From birth to death, they are expected to be inferior, submissive, and timid. I was borned to served rather than be served '.She unleashed all her frustration, humiliation, suffering and then take a long pause as she was free, independent like a bird, who for several years was trapped in the cage and now embark on the journey of salvation, freedom, and liberty. That joy, happiness, cheerfulness was overbound. His husband was stunned and surprised by the new side of her wife personality. His callousness, hostility, malignity towards his wife was shooked away like a dog runs away in terror and awe, beaten or scared by people. That was the end of tolerance which was unfruitful for a soul, for a spirit who encapsulates the unbearable suffering of patriarchal society.

Shefali Lal

Lemons are Sweet

'But Mom, I want to participate in beauty contest which is going to be held in college, doesn't matter whether I should win or not but I don't want to lose this golden opportunity, for exploring my inner worth '.Linda, a girl of 20 yrs, was insisting her mother who was busy in ironing clothes and trying best unheard the conversation between her and daughter.

Linda Fernandes, lives with her mother and brother Paul, who was only 5 yrs old. Linda's father Peter left her mother when she was in the womb of her for another woman. Her mother Anne, work hard to meet the requirements of the family. At the time of her pregnancy, she works in double shifts. From 9 to 2

PM, she teaches in school, and after that she switches her profession from teacher to Nanny of Mrs. Joseph new born baby, who was now Linda's classmate. At the time of joining, She was not considered because as she was her skin was not wholly white. When the family of Mrs. Joseph saw her first time, they make crooked eyes.

'So it's a 1st job of yours or you worked somewhere else'? Mrs. Joseph asked in a indignant voice. 'No, it's my first time, that I putting into the shoes of a nanny. I got separated from my husband, So I have to fulfill the basic amenities of me and for my upcoming baby'. Anne replied in a quiet low voice. The surroundings of house was somewhat gloomy, monotonous for her, Mrs. Joseph class consciousness and anti racist gesture revealing the starking reality of discrimination b/w white and black, that still exist. Nonetheless, Anne was hired by her on the annual salary of 200$. Although, she was quite contented that she become self sufficient, but feeling of loneliness, uneasiness, desolation engulfed her. In new environment, she was always censored, criticized on the basis of color, class, and status. However, Determination, strong will, indomitable confidence of was somewhat inseparable from her.

She worked hard and perform all the responsibilities assigned to her diligently and smartly. Unnecessary complaining, unnecessary pretending ways for the refusal and delaying the work was not her cup of taste. Although, Anne become quite familiar with babysitting, when her own daughter was going to born, she had butterflies in her stomach as she was unhappy with the idea of unbearable labor pain at the time of her delievery.

Linda was born without any complications. When Anne hold her first time, feelings of turbulence, anxiety, sorrow had vanished and converted into the insurmountable happiness. A feeling of joy for becoming a mother was one of the most happiest and imperishable feeling in the world. Little Linda was always feel protected by her mother besides her drunkard father who was ready to knock down this poor, little innocent soul.

Anne, never come to know the meaning of blissfulness, cherished happiness of conjugal life. Every single moment of her life was written with the ink of fear, terror, and violence.Her husband was a monster in the form of human being. His cold hearted, callous, malignant nature turned out her own daughter wavered and provoked. Her childhood was lost, her feelings were never reciprocated, her daughterly attributes seems to be unproductive for his 24/7 full drunkard father. Linda seems to be totally unaware the importance and value of a father in a daughter's life. Perhaps, she developed a stone heart, lack of compassion, pity, sorrow and grief. She stopped crying on her destiny, a destiny which is irrevocable and immutable.

It would be wrong to say that both mother and daughter were subjected to domestic violence but there was another ready to engulf them and that was -Racial discrimination.

When Linda was 13 yrs old and studying in grade 7 th, She was designated with the names 'Black ', 'Negro ', 'Hippy ' by her classmates which ultimately double the emotional turmoil of her. But Linda was manifested with never -dying spirit and unbeatable courage and always ready to rise and shine like a moon who has her own identity .Challenges and complexities of life never and ever broke her, she never gave a chance that she can be easily subdued and bullied. She changed the definition of beauty as she participated in beauty contest and become the 1st non white winner of it, which surprised and amazed even her mother who repeatedly opposed of participating in it.

One day, her mother was making lemonade ,she attentively watched her, when she was cutting the lemons into 2 pieces, she interrupted her and asked

'Mom, why we add sugar or honey into it because lemons have a very tangy sour taste that can minimize the sweetness of sugar'? Anne little bit perplexed but answered that question' I can really sense that my daughter has been grown up now, and become curious and inquisitive to know even the little minor things. Anyway, You know our taste buds always catches the sweet things first, And second thing is that its our perception, our thought process to see the things.

It's not mandatory or compulsory that sour always decrease or minimize the sweet or vice versa. Similarly it is applicable in human life also.Life has two phases :Happiness and Sorrow. Neither happiness exists permanent nor sorrow, it keeps changing and moving. So it depends on us that how we adapt ourselves according to situation. Undoubtedly lemons are sour, but by dissolving in a sugar solution it's give a heavenly and apertive taste.

✍ Shefali Lal

Thank you for reading

Thank you so much for reading this book. Don't forget to give your valuable feedback about this book in the Review section. Also, rate this book between 1 to 5 stars and support us. You can directly contact to author and publisher with the email given below.

Author: lal634005@gmail.com

www.ingramcontent.com/pod-product-compliance
Lightning Source LLC
LaVergne TN
LVHW031244190726
843493LV00010B/3002